Charles Moore

Charles Moore

BY GERALD ALLEN

MONOGRAPHS ON CONTEMPORARY ARCHITECTURE

WHITNEY LIBRARY OF DESIGN, an imprint of Watson-Guptill Publications/New York

GRANADA London Toronto Sydney New York

Copyright © 1980 by Gerald Allen

First published 1980 in New York by Whitney Library of Design,
an imprint of Watson-Guptill Publications,
a division of Billboard Publications, Inc.,
1515 Broadway, New York, N.Y. 10036

Library of Congress Cataloging in Publication Data
Allen, Gerald.
    Charles Moore.
    (Monographs on contemporary architecture)
    1. Moore, Charles Willard, 1925–   2. Archi-
tecture, Modern—20th century—United States.
I. Series.
NA737.M65A84   728'.092'4   80-18247
ISBN 0-8230-7375-0

First published in Great Britain 1981 by Granada Publishing
Granada Publishing—Technical Books Division
Frogmore, St Albans, Herts AL2 2NF
and
3 Upper James Street, London W1R 4BP
117 York Street, Sydney, NSW 2000, Australia
PO Box 84165, Greenside, 2034 Johannesburg, South Africa
61 Beach Road, Auckland, New Zealand
ISBN 0-246-11503-3
Granada®
Granada Publishing®

Manufactured in U.S.A.

First Printing, 1980

Edited by Sharon Lee Ryder and Susan Davis
Designed by Vienne + Lehmann-Haupt

Contents

ACKNOWLEDGMENTS

Architecture books depend at least as much on their pictures as their words, and so the author would like especially to thank Emay Buck, archivist for Moore Grover Harper, Architects in Essex, Connecticut, and Susan Davis of the Whitney Library of Design for their help in securing the graphic materials for this book.

Introduction

On the Road
to the
Palace
of Wisdom

"I like being an outsider," Charles Moore once said to me, after I had asked why at least a part of him seemed uncomfortable in a traditional, established architectural practice with a train of established and influential clients. His remark was surprising to me, since for an outsider he seemed to have an impressive number of built buildings to his credit—now over a hundred by my count. Also he has made a reputation for himself as an architect and teacher that is at the moment close to worldwide, and more important even than that, he has been and still is a powerful influence on several generations of young architects and architecture students. Not bad for an outsider.

But he was right. His remark was not just false modesty but a special statement of past history and present fact. Part of its truth has to do with personality. Born in Michigan, he roamed as a child to Florida and southern California with his peripatetic family who were fleeing the cold winters for months at a time. Away from schools during these protracted jaunts, he was nonetheless brilliantly educated, mainly by himself. He has described himself as something between "Litmus paper and a piranha fish." Largely by reading and listening, he seems to have assimilated the really extensive collection of information which he sports to this day, plus something else still more unusual, particularly among architects: an elegant verbal fluency, the ability to use words profusely and with wit as well as precision. Graphic fluency developed early too, for he has sometimes diffidently described how he stood in front of his classmates in architecture school solving with aplomb a treacherous sketch problem that had thrown the rest into a panic. It was,

no doubt, easy for him.

He must have gained a passionate, childlike daring from this learning process; it is still one of his most important qualities. A similarly intense confidence must have been bred by its successes. Back home in high school and later at the University of Michigan and at Princeton, where he was more formally educated, he could well have regarded the formal yoke of pedagogy to which others had been subjected but which he had managed to escape with a strange mixture of awe and irony. In these environments it must have dawned on him that he was an outsider, albeit an extraordinarily gifted one. He probably relished this position and was not willing to give it up. When he became dean of the Yale Architecture School, he dressed very conservatively but was radically barbered, with a handle-bar mustache that went on to become sideburns. He was not just professional but also funny, outrageous, and kind. His nickname changed from Chuck, the West Coast version, to Charley. Chuck, he said, "lacked class." But what about Charley?

An important architect for much of the past two decades—"an insider playing at being an outsider," a mutual friend of ours once called him—Charles Moore has worked and flourished in a rich and sometimes bizarre environment outside the usual boundaries of professionally cherished norms. It is hard to imagine that his choice of this playing field was not at least willful if not altogether conscious, and suggesting this does not imply that the result is unprofessional, only that it is differently conceived and

Bonham House, Boulder Creek, California.

subsequently not born of a calm and calculatedly efficient architectural machine. It comes instead out of a life of minimum regularity and maximum of bumps and grinds. For an architect famous as a designer of houses, he has spent poignantly little time actually living in one. He has had many offices but works with regularity in none of them. His is a life of almost never being in one place long, of late-night airplane flights, of early-morning meetings, of hurried meals with friends, and of very many things left quite to chance.

In his work, if not in his life, chance is welcomed and embraced: a ridiculously small budget, a cantankerous client, an awkward formal juxtaposition resolved not by dodging but by celebrating it. Sent to hell in flames during a presentation to clients, he is known to have redesigned whole projects on tracing paper before their eyes—just as he did in school.

Leaving things, both social and professional, to chance naturally involves risks and a considerable degree of self-confidence and daring. But it also, after all, presents countless opportunities, chances of another sort. Happily the gambles often pay off in Charles Moore's work, not, in my opinion, in the development of some foolishly consistent theoretical view of the built world, but in a dazzling demonstration of the virtues of taking risks in the first place, of grasping the fleeting opportunity to describe life's variety in buildings. Charles Moore claims that the required state for doing this is one of being "vulnerable"; it involves "caring about the specific things you find, and find out about, so much that you will change your position to accommodate them."[1]

Vulnerable, chancy, risky. All these may seem portentous words to describe an architecture so antic and so arcane as Charles Moore's—buildings that at first appear cheap and chaotic, buildings so thin you could drive a Volkswagen through them, buildings that hauntingly tease most architects' notions of what architecture is. "Say I design like anyone," Philip Johnson is said to have said, "but don't say

I design like Charles Moore."

Such words may also seem inappropriate to apply to the mere making of buildings of any sort. Perhaps they are. But the assumption here is that architecture—like any of the other arts or like science or philosophy—is a means of exercising the human faculty of curiosity and satisfying the human urge to understand. It is one attempt to make life itself intelligible and, with any luck beyond that, meaningful. At its best architecture is, like all these other efforts, serious business. "If architects are to continue to do useful work on this planet," Charles Moore has said, "then surely their proper concern must be the creation of *place*—the ordered imposition of man's self on specific locations across the face of the earth. To make a place is to make a domain that helps people know where they are and, by extension, know who they are."[2]

When Charles Moore told me that he thought he was an outsider, and that he liked being one, it stuck in my mind not just because the confession at first seemed curious and then right, but also because it came very close to meaning the same thing as another word I had already been thinking of to characterize his work. The word was "pastoral." In the tradition of literature, pastoral has had to do with nymphs and shepherds and therefore with countrified things as opposed to citified things and their more organized and frantic pursuit. Charles Moore's buildings seemed to me pastoral in the first place because they did not seem very citified—the work of a man from the country, an outsider. They were on the whole quite small, and many of them seemed to have a seat-of-the-pants quality that eschewed the refinements of high art and high technology, qualities with which architects have lately been preoccupied. Also, like nymphs and shepherds, they were whimsical, the children of fancy, offering capricious and odd-looking versions of the types they actually were.

But there is another reason, too, why Charles Moore's work seemed pastoral, and it is a more important one. At the same time it is countrified it is also highly urbane.

Pastoral poems, it is important to remember, are not the work of simple rustic folk; they are not vernacular. They are written by refined and sophisticated poets. They always deal with the imaginary, and sometimes actual, retreat of worldly people to the country and its simplicities.

Splendid versions of pastoral in English are Shakespeare's early, merry comedies. These almost always begin with people who are troubled by the social, moral, or political perplexities of the courts and cities where they live, and these people are almost always vexed as well by the vagaries of the ultimate perplex, love. So they retreat to a sylvan landscape to find its compensatory solaces, and they do find it, like the exiled Duke in *As You Like It*:

And this our life, exempt from public haunt,
Finds tongues in trees, books in the running brooks,
Sermons in stones, and good in everything. [3]

In the forest, though, strange things begin to happen. Men appear with heads of animals. Girls are mistaken for boys,

boys for girls. Two pairs of lovers fall out of love with each other and into love with their lovers' counterparts. Fairies appear and fly right round the world in the twinkling of an eye. Everything becomes tentative and unhinged; the usual controls on the perceived world are released, and the result is a reverie like the one simple Bottom describes in *A Midsummer Night's Dream*. "The eye of man hath not heard," —his control of metaphor has vanished too—"the ear of man hath not seen, man's hand is not able to taste, his tongue to conceive, nor his heart to report what my dream was."[4]

Late in these plays the revels come to an end. Girls are girls again, boy are boys, and animals animals. The fairies disappear. Miraculously, though—and I think it is meant to be believed as really a miracle, wrought out of the imagination and, as we shall see, of the festival of comic release—the troubles that plagued the players when they came into the forest have disappeared as well, "melted into air, into thin air."[5]

Moore Rogger Hofflander Condominium, Los Angeles.

Courtyard of Moore House, Centerbrook, Connecticut.

Fat Banner by Charles Moore and Christine Beebe.

The mood of the whole exercise is comic, not just because it is funny but also because it ends well. The ritual being dramatized is this: childlike misbehavior ("misrule" it used to be called) leads to release and release leads to clarification. Misrule comes from abandoning the city in the first place and, beyond that, from abandoning the normal precepts through which the world is understood. Release comes from reveling in these abandonments. The miracle, though, is clarity. It is achieved through a fresh understanding of the relationship between people and nature—their own nature as well as the physical world's. Initially perplexed by troubles, these characters proceed, to allude to a favorite quotation of Charles Moore from T. S. Eliot, from a vexed order "in" reality to a restorative understanding of a larger encompassing order, the order "of" reality.[6]

It has been noted that the pastoral ritual of misrule, release, and clarification has its paradigms not just in the saturnalian tradition of classical literature but also in the now mainly vanished tradition of ribald folk holidays in England.[7] There were once many of these, and they were presided over by a festooned emcee, the Lord of Misrule. May Day is the most obvious contemporary descendant. On these holidays misrule was initiated, just as the word says, by abandoning the rules. Of "a hundred maids going to the wood over night," one observer in the 16th century reported on May Day, "there have scarcely the third part of them returned home again undefiled."[8]

By pointing out that these festivals have to do with the idea of pastoral, and by implying that that in turn has to do with the architecture of Charles Moore, I know I am risking the conclusion that the latter is involved with rape. I will settle for saying that it involves misrule, rape's social essence. Examples are numerous: a sophisticated little house with a tar paper roof (tar paper?), a bath tub plonked in the middle of a living room (why not?), windows that look like a waterfall. Once we designed a painted-on version of a window in Giulio Romano's Palazzo del Té for a blank concrete block wall courtyard in Charles Moore's house in

Tower One in New Haven by Charles Moore and the Knights of Columbus Building by Kevin Roche and John Dinkeloo.

Centerbrook, Connecticut. "Tee-Hee Palace" we called it and felt satisfied. But then he did it one better: a "fat banner" on which Giulio's rusticated surround was not painted but quilted, and the rusticated quilts also became curtains in the window itself, complete with tiebacks. All this, I am saying, is pastoral.

Another aspect of pastoral, and therefore of Charles Moore's work, is that in its misrule it is not just a denial of the orderly and rational pursuits of the world, not just a childlike rejection. It is also a subtle parody of them.[9] In some unruly and slightly disturbing way it is actually *like* them, not different. And this implication, of course, teeters breathtakingly on the suggestion that misrule and rule, indiscretion and discretion, disorder and order are not opposites but parts of a whole which one can dare to admit and dare to comprehend.

A clear example of pastoral parody is the *Second Shepherds' Play*, an anonymous 15th-century work whose action consists of two plots juxtaposed. The first involves a man who steals a lamb, wraps it in swaddling clothing and hides it in a cradle. The second plot involves the nativity of Christ, the birth of the lamb of God who is cradled in a manger. In tone the play splits decisively down the middle into two parts, one rowdy and one sacred. But in theme the division is not quite so clear. The comic first part serves not just to make us ask, "What is this?" It also does something more: by being so tantalizing like its sacred opposite in several respects, it forces us to ask a more difficult question, "What is *that*?"

Charles Moore's buildings seem to me filled with instructive parodies of this kind. In New Haven, his elderly housing tower, when seen from just the right angle, appears as big as Kevin Roche and John Dinkeloo's actually much bigger Knights of Columbus Building across the freeway, only it is bereft of the latter's big cylindrical corners. The question thus posed is not so much why Charles Moore's building does not have them as why Roche and Dinkeloo's

University of California Faculty Club, Santa Barbara.

does—which turns out in fact not to be an unreasonable thing to wonder about. The ebullient—others have called it just plain tacky—Faculty Club for the University of California at Santa Barbara boasts moose heads on the walls, garish neon banners, plus a real crystal chandelier in questionable taste—all there as parodies of grander (are we meant to note that they are also stuffier) private clubs. And there is, of course, his really ribald version of classical architecture in the Piazza d'Italia in New Orleans, the naughty *chef d'oeuvre* of a Lord of Misrule.

Comedy, misrule, release, and clarification. It does not seem to me extravagant to say that this sequence characterizes the work of Charles Moore, the confessed outsider.

His work is, in a word, pastoral. But by being that it does not merely contradict one set of urbane and citified things with another set of things that are rude and countrified, unruly and excessive. "The road of excess," William Blake once pointed out, "leads to the palace of wisdom."[10] Charles Moore's work offers the shocking, the rowdy, the funny, and the eccentric as paths towards some larger comprehension of the world. It also offers the revitalizing proposition that the language of architecture is rich enough to describe the world fully.

University of California Faculty Club, Santa Barbara.

14

Projects

Bonham House

This little weekend retreat house for a woman who taught school in Berkeley was one of the first buildings by Charles Moore to gain notoriety. It was also one of the first to sound so vividly the festive, comic themes that have since become consistent components of his work: misrule that evokes surprise and release and that leads finally to a new clarification of what a building might be.

The design of the Bonham House flies willfully in the face of most of the presumptions about what an architect-contrived house is. It is not just small, it is veritably tiny (a fact that is somewhat belied by the very wide-angle lenses required to photograph it), and it was not only very inexpensive in terms of budget, but downright cheap in its choice of materials. It revels in them, as it does in the odd and unprecedented shapes that make it up.

Its miracle, for all that, is that in the end it is still a whole thing—recognizable, fresh, and serene.

The house was designed in 1961 by Charles Moore with Warren Fuller and constructed in 1962 in the Santa Cruz Mountains below San Francisco on a hillside shadowed by monumental stands of redwood trees. It was to be used mainly for parties and weekends; the budget was $7,500 (tiny even for 1961), and the program called for 550 square feet (51 square meters) [567 (53 square meters) actually materialized, plus a screened porch]. The house consists of one main room lit by a large industrial steel-and-glass window, shown in the adjacent photograph; it was the cheapest alternative then, though by no means now. On either side of this room are two appendages, hung to it like saddlebags. The one on the left contains the kitchen on the lower level and a bathroom above; the one on the right is the screened porch. The exterior siding is Texture 1-11 plywood stained a soft, gray-green, and the roof is asphalt roll roofing—"tar paper." The chimney is a cheap metal flue; "it kept blowing down in a violent breeze," Moore once reminisced.

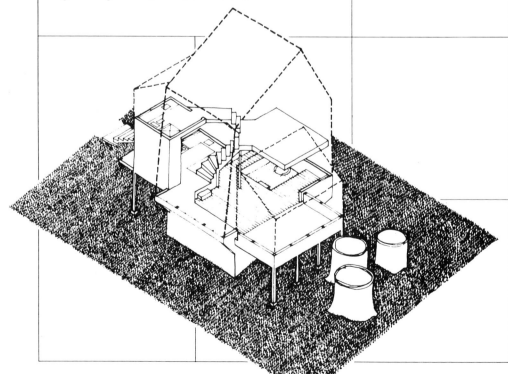

The main room of the
Bonham House, shown in the
photograph on the left, is
barely 14 feet (4.3 meters)
square, though it tries to
make up in height for part of
what it lacks in width and
breadth. Still there is almost
no room for furniture, and
so slight changes in level —
up to the window seat and to
the entry to its right and
down to an adjoining fireplace area — make substitute
places to sit and put things.
The higher level near the
entrance also makes
possible a shorter run of
stairs, shown in the photograph on the opposite page,
to the bedroom loft above
the fireplace. The interior
walls are of plywood, usually painted white so the
dappled light through the
large windows, and through
the redwoods beyond, can
play brightly on them.

Hubbard House

The Hubbard House, designed about two years before the Bonham House shown on the previous pages, is less well known and exudes a less spontaneous brio than it and other later works by Charles Moore. Once described in print as a "serene and unassertive builder home," it is included here because it was designed as a single but nonetheless important part of an overall housing development scheme and because with its low and brooding pyramidal roof topped by a square, flat clerestory it recalls more monumental architectural shapes at a domestic scale.

For both reasons it signals concerns that were soon to become more dramatically evident in Charles Moore's work—in terms of monumental recollection, his own house in Orinda three years later, and in terms of that and also of large-scale planning of the buildings at the Sea Ranch, the first of which was designed some two years later still.

Designed in 1959 by Charles Moore with Richard C. Peters and built in 1960, the house was a pilot project, the first in a subdivision of one-acre lots adjoining a newly completed country club between Monterey and Salinas, California. It was to have a powerful identity, to establish a standard for future houses in the development, and to appeal to a wide variety of future buyers, living formally or informally, with young or no children, with or without servants. It was built by Roy Hubbard, a previous house client of the architect; hence the name. The site is a level mesa which at its extreme southern edge drops abruptly to the valley floor. There are steady and often strong winds from the northwest, and so the house, which faced north, is protected by a fenced entrance court. Generous decks on the other side, facing a superb view, are shielded by the house itself.

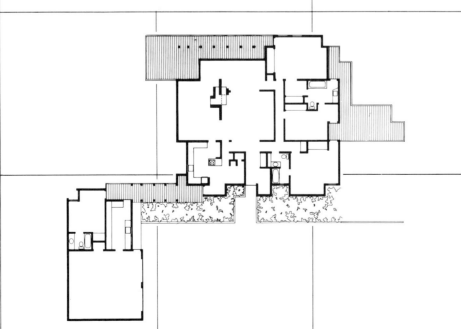

Inside the house, the central living space can either be furnished as a formal area or flow more informally into the space beyond it, which opens in turn onto the deck. Similarly, the space on the other side of the chimney can function either as a dining room or as a family room.

One of the bedrooms can double as a study, another as a servant's room.

Moore House, Orinda

Once when a critic had railed against the frivolous and socially offensive meanings he had found in one of Charles Moore's houses, the architect fired back, "It's a house, not a hair shirt." Well, maybe. But if Charles Moore's houses are not hair shirts, they usually are not just houses either, as this one he built for himself shows. Its forms admittedly derive from primitive huts and from Mayan or Hindu temples—to say nothing of the famous Trenton Bathhouses by Louis I. Kahn—and Moore makes it clear that he was thinking in broad and recollective terms when he made the design.

"Years before, a bulldozer had cut a flat circular building site, which had since grown grassy and now seemed part of the natural setting, like those perfectly circular meadows that inspired medieval Chinese poets to meditate upon perfection."[1] Freed, since he was a bachelor, from most of the usual programmatic constraints, Moore reveled in that freedom and in the pursuit of a primitive, mythic expression of the idea of a house.

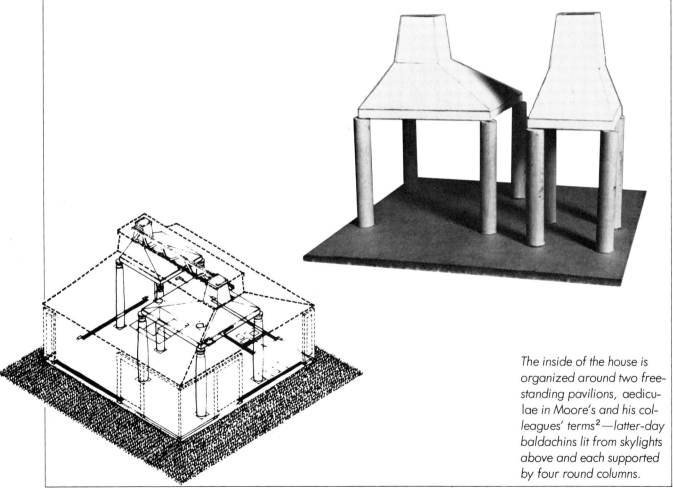

The inside of the house is organized around two free-standing pavilions, aediculae in Moore's and his colleagues' terms[2]—latter-day baldachins lit from skylights above and each supported by four round columns.

Charles Moore's house in Orinda, California, was designed and built in 1962. Light enters through the pavilions, whose insides are painted white; through the top of the main roof, which is stained dark and is therefore dim; and through the corners of the house, where sliding barn doors open to the oak woods outside. In one case this plunges the piano into what the architect describes as "a kind of exhilarating jeopardy."[3]

The outside walls of the house never come to the corners, and the roof springs from a perimeter beam on top of them. It is then supported by the columns of the two pavilions below. All that comes to the ground are the eight columns, the fixed parts of the outside walls, and several walls just inside the perimeter that hold shelves and kitchen equipment and enclose a toilet. Beds are positioned around a giant bookshelf between the two pavilions. The furniture is free to arrange itself in changing patterns under and around the larger pavilion. In the smaller pavilion is an outsized sunken bath and shower, a celebration of the once-public act of bathing, liberated here from the usual cramped and conventional bathroom.

Sea Ranch Condominium

The urge to surprise and be different, the urge to create at small scale monumental architectural recollections, and the urge to be a part of the planning of a larger environment—all these are present in Charles Moore's earlier work. And all these coalesce vividly in the famous Sea Ranch Condominium, whose completion marked the beginning of the first major phase of his career as an architect.

The condominium also appeared at a time when it seems many people were ready to see its architectural concerns embodied, and so the building became one of the most influential of its decade; it was published, studied, talked about, photographed, visited—and copied. It helped change the face of American architecture.

The surprises that the Sea Ranch Condominium proffered undoubtedly came from the fact that it forthrightly ignored a good many of the rubrics of architecture up to that point in the 20th century. A significant exception was the work of the Finn Alvar Aalto, himself something of an outsider in Modernist architectural circles, and in particular his famous town hall at Saynatsaalo, which is the most obvious single antecedent of the condominium at the Sea Ranch.

The image, though, is Californian, and the recollection it stirs is of old barns and country industrial structures— "mineshaft modern," its critics called it. The image, too, is written large, using a technique that had been traditional in housing design until the advent of the Modern Movement: individual units are gathered up together, losing some of their own identity, to create an overall architectural entity. Richard Morris Hunt once said of his Biltmore House in the Blue Ridge that "the mountains are in scale with the house."[1] The Sea Ranch Condominium, for its part, is in scale with the somber north coast.

Its planning concerns are double-edged. Any building at the Sea Ranch, of which this was one of the first, should not spoil the splendid, desolate landscape; at the same time this very landscape was going to be developed. What was therefore required was an effort to be sensitive to the natural environment and, at the same time, set up a series of procedures for building other buildings there.

The attempt ultimately was not a complete success, and the fact that it was not should be a perplexing concern of any architect who wants to influence the built environment beyond the lot lines of his own work.

In the end, "those same media-driven winds which blew the 'Sea Ranch idiom' abroad and made it famous," Charles Moore has said, "also blew uncaring versions of Swiss chalets and splitlevels to this splendid brooding coast." "But we guessed wrong, too," he adds. "We sought a partnership of buildings with the vast landscape which required more presence than most houses have and more care in the arrangements than most people working somewhere else chose to give."[2]

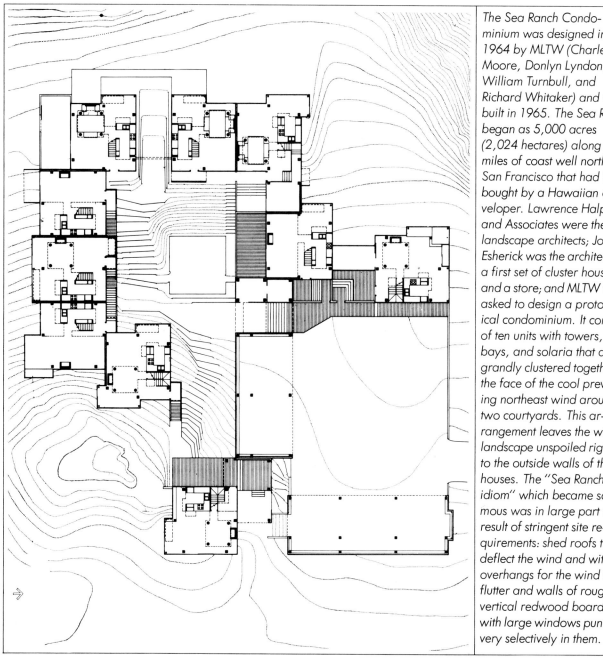

The Sea Ranch Condominium was designed in 1964 by MLTW (Charles Moore, Donlyn Lyndon, William Turnbull, and Richard Whitaker) and was built in 1965. The Sea Ranch began as 5,000 acres (2,024 hectares) along 10 miles of coast well north of San Francisco that had been bought by a Hawaiian developer. Lawrence Halprin and Associates were the landscape architects; Joseph Esherick was the architect for a first set of cluster houses and a store; and MLTW were asked to design a prototypical condominium. It consists of ten units with towers, bays, and solaria that are grandly clustered together in the face of the cool prevailing northeast wind around two courtyards. This arrangement leaves the wild landscape unspoiled right up to the outside walls of the houses. The "Sea Ranch idiom" which became so famous was in large part the result of stringent site requirements: shed roofs to deflect the wind and with no overhangs for the wind to flutter and walls of rough vertical redwood boards with large windows punched very selectively in them.

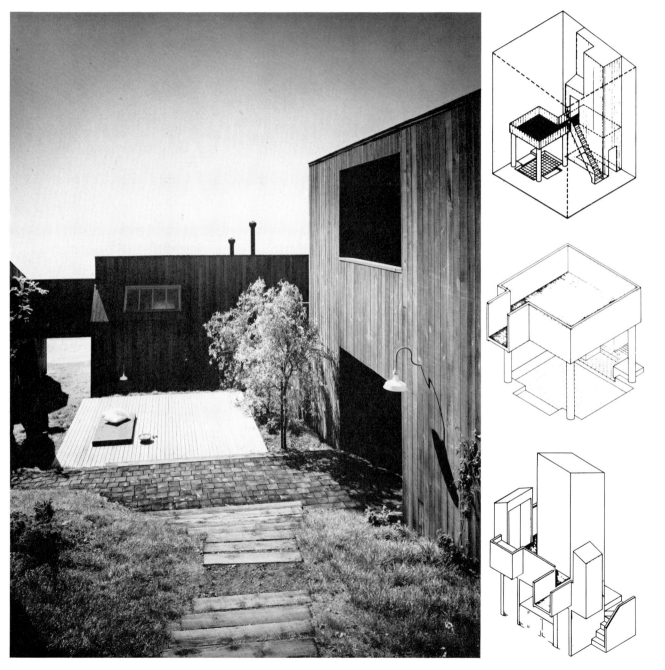

Though the Sea Ranch is relatively free from the fog in which most of the north coast is often shrouded, the cool wind is almost constant, and so the problem is to get out of the wind and into the sun, as in the enclosed courtyard shown on the left. Each of the condominium units consists of a single large room with appended bays and porches—a variation on the scheme for the little Bonham House shown on pages 16–19. Inside each great room are usually two free-standing "houses," bigger than furniture, but not so big as a real building. One is a four-poster pavilion—a variation of the aediculae in Moore's own house in Orinda (pages 24–29)—that shelters a fireplace below and provides a sleeping loft above. The other contains a kitchen below, stairs, a bath and dressing room above, and sometimes another sleeping loft above that.

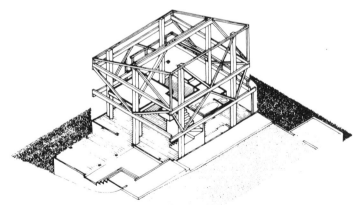

The condominiums are of old-fashioned post-and-beam redwood construction. The adjacent photograph shows the fireplace beneath a four-poster pavilion and, beyond that, a series of bays that hang outside the perimeter of the single great redwood room, providing extra places for sitting or sleeping or for being conceptually "outside" the house and near the view of the ocean. The photograph above also shows the same pavilion, but beyond it is an appended solarium.

Sea Ranch Swim Club I

E dith Wharton once said that there were only two ways of dealing with a room that was fundamentally ugly: "one is to accept it, and the other is courageously to correct its ugliness."[1] A third would be to add supergraphics, since little courage is required, only some paint, a brush, and an eye.

The interiors of the first Sea Ranch Swim Club are by no means ugly, but just as the Sea Ranch Condominium seems to have captured the fancies of a whole generation of architects, so did the first swim club, largely because of the bold painting of its interior by Barbara Stauffacher, one of the first examples of supergraphics anywhere.

That, plus the startlingly beautiful use of ordinary heat lamps in plain porcelain receptacles and mail boxes for lockers, offered a ready series of possibilities to designers who saw it and were themselves interested in a quick fix. Its simplicities were beguiling, and much of its allure was that it all seemed a great deal easier to do than it actually was.

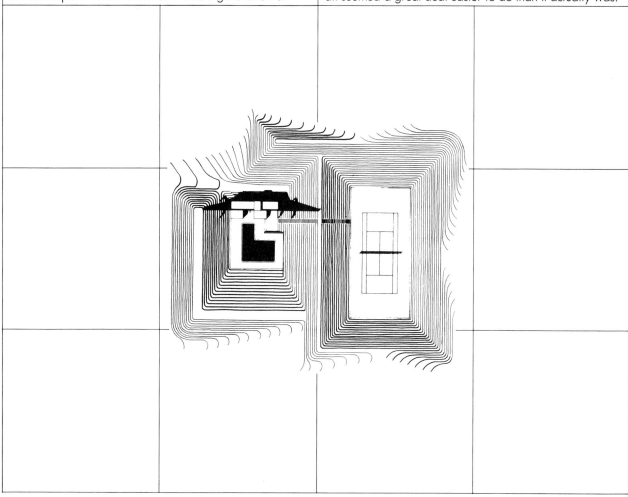

The first Sea Ranch Swim Club was designed by MLTW/Moore-Turnbull in 1966 and built in the same year. The pool and tennis court were designed by Lawrence Halprin and Associates. Like the condominium, this building is in the path of the prevailing winds, and so the swimming pool and tennis courts are dug into the ground and surrounded by earth berms. On the windward side of the pool, the small building containing the changing rooms is actually a long wooden wall against the wind, with tiny spaces inside lit from above by translucent plastic roofs.

Johnson House

The bluffs along the 10-mile shore at the Sea Ranch form a coastal plain a few hundred yards wide, and when development began these were interrupted only by rows of fifty-year-old Monterey cypress trees that had been introduced perpendicular to the coast at irregular intervals for wind protection.

Beyond the meadows there was a ridge of low hills covered in forests. The original land-use plan called for large condominiums, like the one by MLTW, along the bluffs, and cluster houses, like the ones designed by Joseph Esherick, nestled against the wind breaks. In the hills, single-family houses were to merge unobtrusively into the trees.

The Johnson House was a first example, and it sits high on a ridge overlooking the shore just where the forest gives way to open meadows and a sweeping view of the Pacific Ocean. Like Charles Moore's earlier Bonham House and his own house in Orinda, it essentially has only one room. To convey at once the sense of being a mansion and a plain shack, it consists of an imposing form built in a simple and unimposing way. A drive through the forest ends at a redwood gate that opens onto a small flowered clearing. On the far side of this sits the house, fitted between a thicket of redwood and one of tanbark oak. From this side, and under its pyramidal roof, it seems like a doll house, a simple geometric form with a central entrance porch.

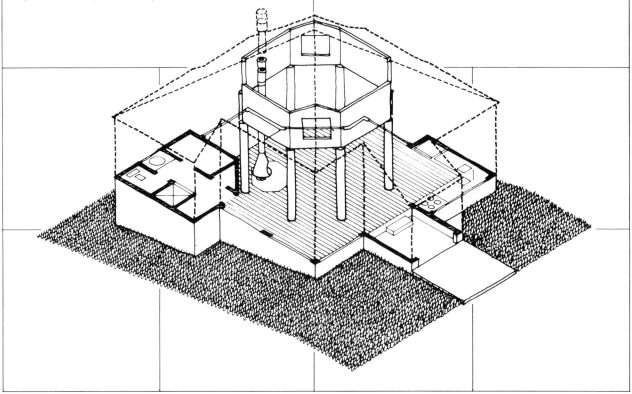

Inside the Johnson House, which was designed by MLTW/Moore-Turnbull in 1965 and built in 1966, one discovers something that the simple exterior did not hint of: a surprising octagonal pavilion reminiscent of great halls, tombs, and bandstands in the park, but supported by plywood "cores," the cylindrical pieces of wood left over when plys have been peeled off in mills, locally available when the house was built for ninety cents each. Between the columns, the space stretches out into individual niches for specific purposes. Directly ahead is a nook for sitting and sleeping, with the fireplace to one side and a view up the coast on the other through a large window that comes right down to the floor. To the immediate right as one enters, the room extends into a corner for kitchen equipment, while on the immediate left, lodged between the columns of the pavilion and the outside walls of the house, is a place for eating, shown on the following page. Behind the fireplace on the far left are a giant closet and a bathroom and dressing room. Skylights just outside the perimeter of the octagon emphasize its shape and make it distinct from the encompassing volume of the house itself, surrounding it with a halo of soft light and with surprising shafts of sunshine. This light from above illuminates the white walls and therefore lessens the glare from the sea and sky, framing the view of the outdoors.

In the Johnson House the connection between use-specific spaces around the perimeter and the central, symbolic space is assured by the open spaces between the columns and, more subtly, by four square openings pierced in the walls of the octagon above. However, the distinction between the two realms is maintained with equal care, for the octagon in the middle is kept separate, never touching the outside walls even when it comes within a few inches of them, as it does behind the fireplace and in front of the large window framing the view. Each of the areas for specific use around the perimeter, as well as the octagon in the center, with its feeling of mock grandeur, is in fact much too small to be functional or effective alone. And so each borrows from the other in this miniature house, and each of the parts therefore performs at least two separate tasks.

Budge House

Every so often in Charles Moore's work a building of almost complete repose appears—serene rather than antic and as relaxed as a lyric poem. The Budge House is one of these, and the Swan House, shown on pages 104—109, is another.

The Budge House was made to stand in an oak forest overlooking a pond north of San Francisco, where it would be used mainly in the summer months, which are still and quiet, and when rain is virtually unknown. The house recalls other very simple houses, like classical farmhouses of California or Japan: a rectangular structure covered by a half-hip, reverse gambrel roof and almost completely encircled by a screened porch to shade the place from the summer sun.

Here most of the walls of the house are made so they fold up against the ceiling of the porch, merging the rooms inside with it—allowing the whole house to become a great porch, a pavilion sitting in the trees. For the cold winter months the walls can be lowered back into place, and the middle of the house—unlike a farmhouse but like a barn—is open to the peak of the roof, where skylights dramatize its center.

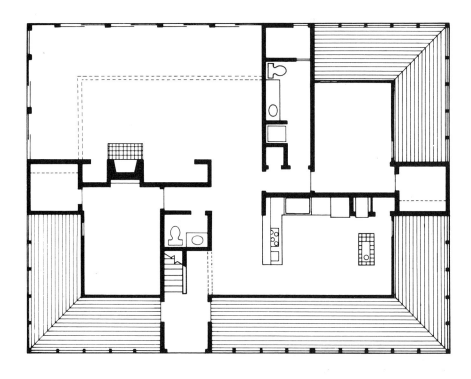

The Budge House was designed in 1966 by MLTW/ Moore-Turnbull and built in 1967 near Healdsburg, California, for a San Francisco lawyer, his wife, and their children as a weekend and summer retreat. In each corner of the rectangular plan is a room —two bedrooms in opposite corners and in the other two a living room and a kitchen. Unlike the other rooms the living room extends all the way to the outer perimeter of the house and is enclosed not by screens but by fixed glass and sliding glass doors, giving it extra space and light even in winter, when the counterbalanced walls in the other rooms are shut down. The living room has a fireplace for these winter days and nights.

Two of the photographs on the opposite page show the kitchen —the upper one with the counterbalanced walls swung up to merge the room with the porch (as shown in detail on the lower right) and the lower left one with the walls down for cool days and nights. The photograph on the right shows the high, skylit center of the house. The spaces on the upper level are sleeping lofts —the one on the left reached by a flight of stairs, the one on the right by a drawbridge under the sky-lights.

Moore House, New Haven

When Charles Moore moved to New Haven to become the head of the Yale Architectural School in 1965, the chance came again to make a house for himself, and "the awesome responsibility of spending other people's money was replaced with the much more relaxed opportunity of spending one's own."[1] Like the house he had built for himself earlier in Orinda, shown on pages 24–29, the one in New Haven is indeed relaxed, eccentric, and, more than any other building he had designed up to that point, fantastical, sporting elements that are traditional, pop, and kitsch—"supermanneristic" the combination later came to be called[2]—in a richly complex spatial arrangement.

The design was a renovation and began with a very small late 19th-century wooden house on a street near the Yale campus. It was, in the architect's opinion, altogether too small, so that merely gutting it would not be enough

because that would merely reveal an inadequate volume tightly contained by four walls, a bottom, and a top. The solution was to gouge out parts of the interior and to insert two-story towers of space—three of them, in fact, named Howard, Berengaria, and Ethel. Each of these towers is made of double-layered plywood walls with large geometric cutouts, often incomplete, that suggest larger geometric orders of which they are a part. Each of them also contains space more or less pure, which contrasts with the tighter spatial arrangement of the rest of the house.

"Space in architecture," Charles Moore has said "—whatever its organizing impulse—is of interest to us in only two ways: either because of its orderly containment or because of the drama of its escape."[3] Faced here with an altogether too orderly version of the former, he opted for a really festive version of the latter.

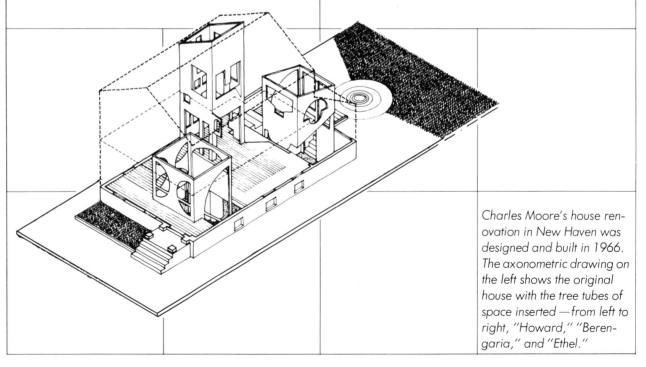

Charles Moore's house renovation in New Haven was designed and built in 1966. The axonometric drawing on the left shows the original house with the tree tubes of space inserted —from left to right, "Howard," "Berengaria," and "Ethel."

The photographs on these pages show *Ethel,* which contains a small breakfast area and opens on one side to the kitchen equipment and on the other to a passage higher up on the main floor level that leads to a garden in the back of the house. The figure peering out the sliding glass door is part of a Volkswagen billboard pasted up on the wall. On the lower level by the breakfast table a pair of classical columns of the composite order, rescued from a demolition site, proved too short to shore up a sagging beam above, and so a pair of adjustable Lally columns have been inserted to aid them in their task.

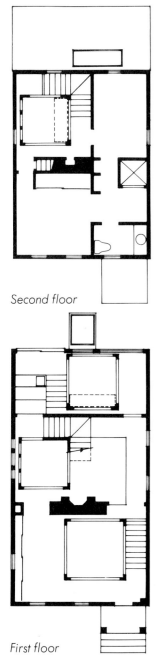

Second floor

First floor

The photograph on the left shows the tower known as "Howard," which plunges from the main floor just inside the entrance to the basement below and to a small desk at which the architect is shown working. Through the double-layered plywood cutout at main floor level can be seen a series of numbers on sliding panels, shown above. The bedroom, with a bed that is something between an old-fashioned four-poster and a Baroque dome, is shown on the right.

Church Street South

"A dwelling should be the center of the universe for people who share it," Charles Moore has said. "To puzzle out a shape for the center of the universe with one interested family is a complex task. But to place dozens, or even hundreds, of these centers together for inhabitation by people whose identities are generally not even known to the designer approaches the hopeless."[1] The Sea Ranch Condominium, shown on pages 30–37, was a first attempt to address this problem, and Church Street South, federally financed housing in New Haven, was the next and more ambitious one. It was designed between 1966 and 1968 by MLTW/Moore-Turnbull with Marvin Buchanan and Donald Whitaker, and the first phase of it was constructed in 1969. It is still incomplete.

A large area in New Haven between downtown and the railroad station had been cleared in the early phases of massive urban renewal. This had been surrounded with Kevin Roche and John Dinkeloo's Lee High School, Knights of Columbus Building, and Coliseum. In the middle, housing was required at a very low budget. The site plan here shows how it is organized to produce a pedestrian approach to the railroad station on the right and the edge of downtown on the left. The photograph above shows a view from one of the courtyards along this pedestrian way looking towards downtown.

Most of the three- and four-story buildings in Church Street South house two-, three-, four-, and five-bedroom apartments for large families. The blocks are repetitious to fit a rigid budget, but the site is designed to create a variety of squares and streets that, it was hoped, might give a sense of location to the almost identical housing units.

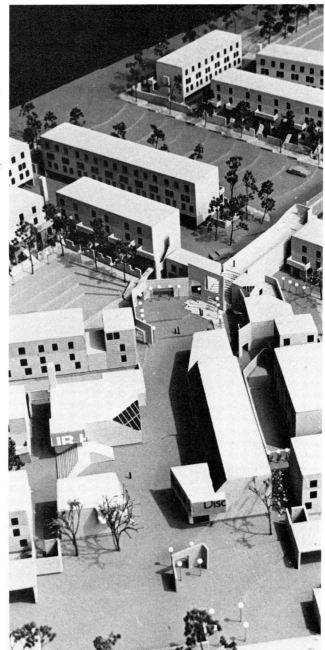

The developers of Church Street South had specified a structural scheme of concrete planking spanning between precast wall slabs, and this required absolutely standard and identical facades. At the last minute, though, concrete blocks were substituted for the precast slabs, since it turned out that they were ultimately cheaper, but too late to vary the facades. And so front entrances were painted to try to give them some variety. The aerial photograph here shows how the housing development attempts to connect the New Haven Railroad Station at the lower right to the elderly housing tower and the Knights of Columbus Building just above that and finally to the New Haven green at the top of the photograph.

Santa Barbara Faculty Club

The Faculty Club for the University of California at Santa Barbara celebrates, according to the architect, "with leaps of scale and waves of incongruities"[1] the traditions of Santa Barbara architecture. It began with Spanish colonization but really flowered, following a disastrous earthquake in 1925, in a partly remembered but largely made-up, ebullient idiom of white stucco walls, low-pitched Mediterranean tile roofs, and gentle silhouettes against the deep blue sky, an Anglo-Californian vision of Spanish romance.

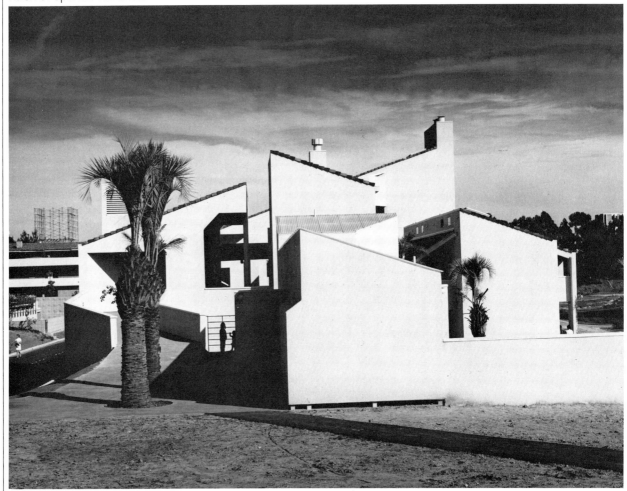

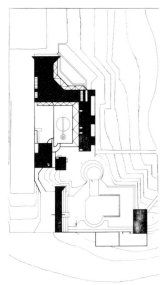

The photograph on the opposite page shows the ramp leading to the main entrance of the Faculty Club; on the right is the large interior courtyard with a fountain made of painted concrete and a lawn sprinkler.

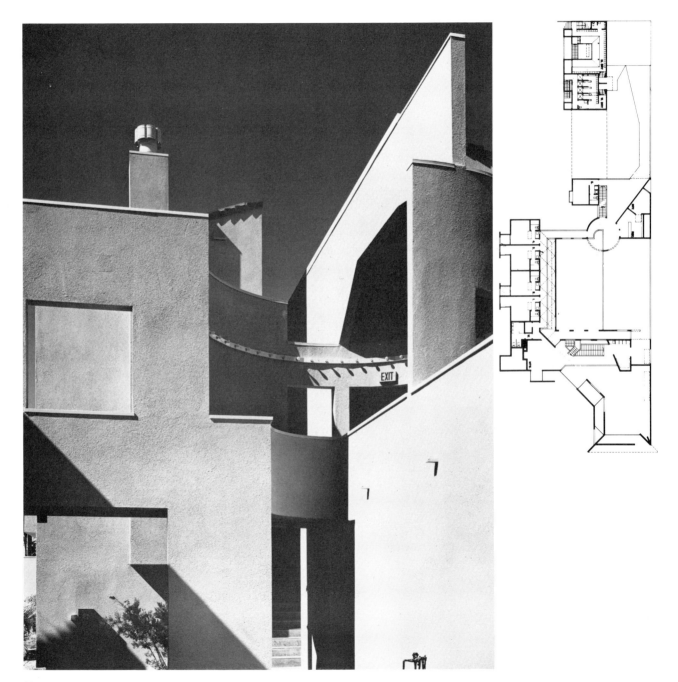

The Faculty Club was designed by MLTW/Moore-Turnbull with Donlyn Lyndon, Marvin Buchanan, and Bruce Beebe in 1966 and constructed in 1968. The photograph on the opposite page shows the circular outdoor foyer through which the entrance path to the club passes, one level above the courtyard shown on the previous page. The photograph above shows the outside of the building near the swimming pool.

The photograph above shows the side of the building that contains the main dining room and faces a small lagoon. The space between the inner and outer walls, buttressed by trusses and shown on the opposite page, is roofed when necessary by corrugated plastic and lit with cool fluorescent lamps. At night these create a 4-foot-thick (1.2-meter) blanket of blue light that contrasts with the warmer incandescent light of the interior.

The main dining room is festooned with antique tapestries, a crystal chandelier, neon banners, and stairways and platforms that zigzag upwards through the high space. A lounge with its antique fireplace surround and the club locker rooms are shown on the opposite page.

Moore House, Centerbrook

When Charles Moore moved his office and his home from New Haven to Centerbrook, Connecticut, in 1970, the chance came for him to indulge himself with particular abandon in one of his lifelong fascinations: collecting and more particularly displaying the collection in profusion. "By surrounding yourself with things that have special meaning for you, which you have chosen from among other similar things," he has said, "you can add dimension to the place you inhabit and to its capacity to nurture your imagination."[1] "It is a possibility," he adds, "that was angrily excluded by many Modern architects who insisted that lilies were not for gilding."[2]

In the game of collecting, though, all is lost if the resulting collection is not personal, something which Charles Moore vividly demonstrated in his house in Centerbrook. Displayed there are books, Mexican saints, toy soldiers, funny clocks, birdcages, wolf skins, and a chic Italian light that snakes across a bed. This is not collecting in the sense of the art gallery world or the world of interior designer, and the fact that few of the objects are "fine" in those terms renders the point more poignantly: a collection is finally worthless if it is not personal.

Charles Moore's house in Centerbrook is a renovation of an old office next to a factory building, which now houses one of his several architectural offices. It was designed and built from 1970 to 1975.

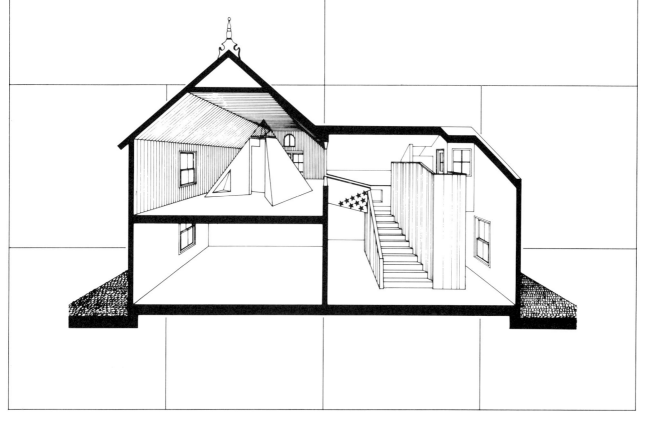

On the lower floor of Moore's renovation in Centerbrook are spaces for a sitting room and library and, shown on the left, a dining area with a small kitchen concealed in the stairway that leads to the upper floor and a bed-sitting room. The pyramid that houses the bed and a small closet is modeled on the Great Seal of the United States, which appears on the dollar bill, and on the Great Pyramid of Giza, with its honeycombed interior presided over in this version by hoards of marching toy soldiers.

Koizim House

The Koizim House was designed during the heyday of pop architecture, of supergraphics, and of the 45-degree angle. And so it shows how all these fashionable ways of approaching the design of a building were combined with other ways, how they were refined, and how indeed they began to lose some of their punch when they were no longer applied to rough-and-ready buildings like those at the Sea Ranch, shown on pages 30–47, but were instead translated into the context of a large and expensive house.

The house is memorable as well for being, in the mind's eye at least, not just a single building but a whole cluster of separate little plaster houses, a village. Between these are high, irregular spaces thought of as enclosed porches, and in the middle of them is a large and glassy living space, an interior village square. The house was designed in 1969 by MLTW/Moore-Turnbull with Arthur Ballman and built in Westport, Connecticut, in 1971.

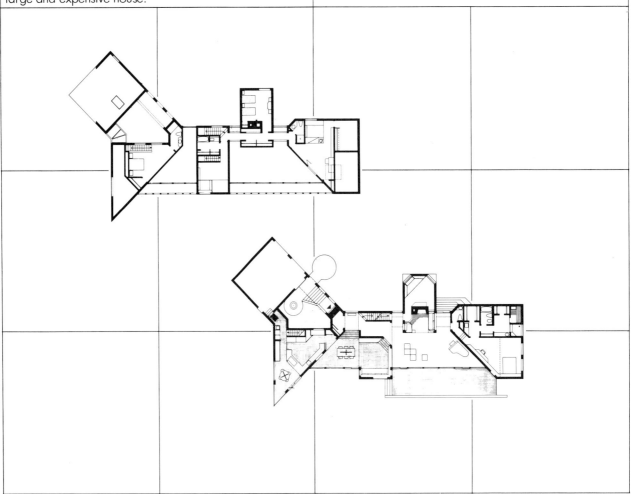

The plans show how the house is conceived of as a collection of intimately scaled little houses. Between them are the high, bright spaces for living and dining. Mylar-covered bridges connect the little houses on the upper level. The photograph above shows the entrance.

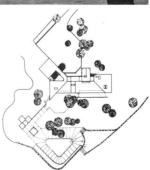

The photograph on the left shows the back, glassy side of the Koizim House, which opens onto a lawn and Long Island Sound beyond. The photograph on the right shows this view from the living room.

The main space between the individual stucco "houses" that make up the Koizim House is the living room; it opens at one end to a bedroom, at the other to a dining area, and along one side to a low, sheltered nook in front of the fireplace. The photograph on the right shows the front vestibule as it opens into the dining area; the ornate valance that marks the transition is made of key rings and key chains.

Xanadune

A favorite formal technique of Charles Moore is to cover a series of intricate and complex spaces with a large pyramidal roof draped over them like a huge tent. The Johnson House at the Sea Ranch, shown on pages 42–47, is an early but not the first example, and the Koizim House, shown on the six preceding pages, is a variation. One of the clearest examples is the project Xanadune — condominiums designed for St. Simons Island in Georgia. From a distance the building indeed appears to be all roof and dormers, and only on closer inspection do the intricacies appear: a series of individual condominium units wrapped about a richly configured interior courtyard.

This design also shows how by the early 1970s Charles Moore's work was recalling much more than before, and much more specifically, not just the forms of historical architecture but the shapes as well. Xanadune was designed in 1972 by Charles W. Moore Associates with Richard Oliver, Mary Ann Rumney, and Robert Yudell.

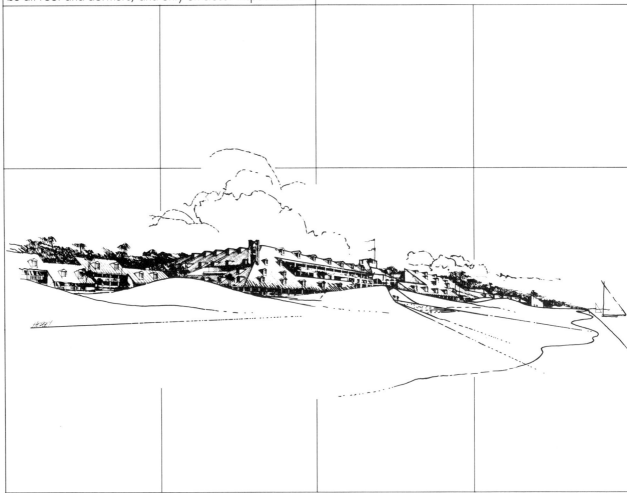

The drawing on the opposite page shows the condominiums as seen from the shore with their shapes reminiscent of giant oceanfront hotels in places like Cape May and San Diego. The model above and the sections on the right show how this overall, singular impression becomes more complex in the arrangements of the individual parts: seven basic unit types on as many as five floors are grouped into three basic building types around the central courtyard.

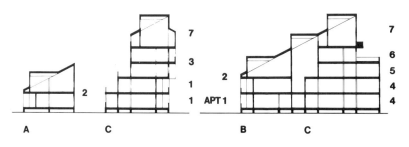

The model for Xanadune is shown on the left, and above and right are views through the interior courtyard of the project, with its swimming pool, gazebo, and fountains.

Burns House

The Burns House was designed for an urban planner who teaches at the University of California at Los Angeles, and he brought at least two specific requirements to it. The building should reflect the patterns and traditions of life in southern California, and it also had to house a fine baroque pipe organ of which the client is the fortunate owner.

The result is a series of sheds and towers, not unlike Charles Moore's work some ten years earlier at the Sea Ranch, but here clothed in more regionally apposite stucco in many shades of ochre, orange, and mauve. The house is on the side of a steeply sloping canyon built on a platform that is barely 75 feet (23 meters) square. On the uphill side is the entrance; on the downhill side, which is seen below, the house opens to a terrace with a swimming pool and a view. Inside is a special room for the organ which can be closed off from the rest of the house with the sliding wooden doors at the right of the photograph on the opposite page.

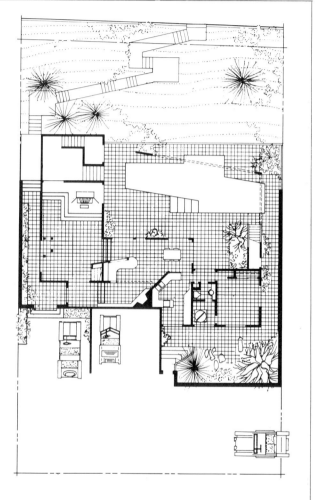

The section perspective of the Burns House here is taken looking from the entrance side downhill to the pool just outside the glass doors on the first level. The organ room is on the left. In the middle, and down several steps, is a sitting area with additional room for dining. A guest room is on the right on this level. On the next level up is the master bedroom and bath, and above that is a study, reached from both the inside and outside by flights of stairs.

The Burns House was designed in 1972 by Charles Moore with Richard Chylinski and was built in 1974 in Santa Monica, California. Colors were chosen by Christine Beebe, and lighting was designed by Richard C. Peters. The swimming pool on the right opens out to a view of the canyon in which the house is built.

The photograph on the left is taken from the organ room in the Burns House looking out to the stairway that leads to the master bedroom on the second level and continues on to the study on the third. The sitting area and dining area can be seen in the lower left of the photograph, and the former is shown on the opposite page.

A House near New York

During the writing of *The Place of Houses*, Stratford Hall, the 18th-century Virginia mansion, kept appearing over and over as an example of various principles of house building. Stratford appeared still again in the design of this large house near New York, this time as the loose formal model for the three pavilions, capped by chimneys and belvederes, around which the house is organized.

But here the resemblance stops, and a more obvious model can be found in Charles Moore's own Koizim House, shown on pages 78– 83. There a series of more or less discrete pavilions are clustered together and the spaces in between become free-flowing, conceptually outside the rest but still actually indoors. The central space in this house near New York is a large orangerie, shown in the photograph on the opposite page.

This house was designed by Charles Moore and Richard B. Oliver in 1973 and built in 1976; Christine Beebe was the color consultant.

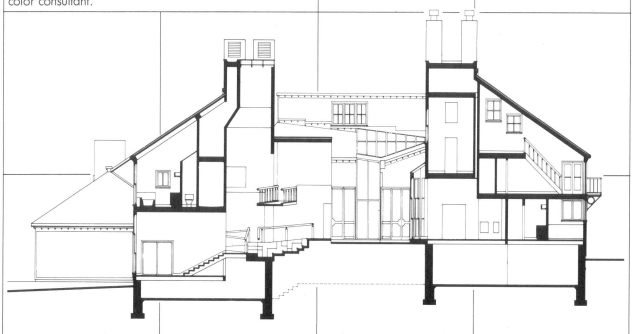

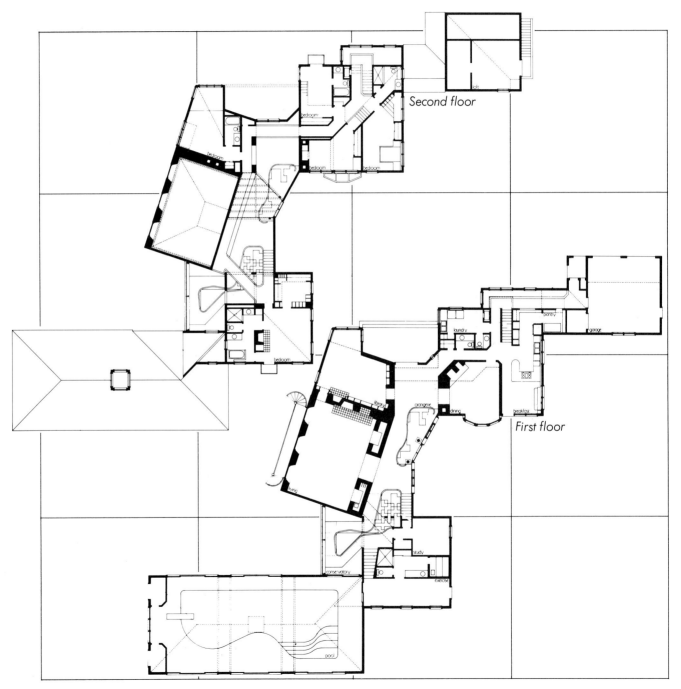

Second floor

First floor

This rural house was designed for an owner who is blind and his wife and children, who are sighted. The program called for discrete rooms, acoustical clarity, and also an ease of movement. At the heart of the house is an indoor garden, an orangerie whose fountain, flowers, and continuous handrailings give aural, olifactory, and tactile clues —as well as visual ones —to its nature.

The largest discrete space in the house is the living room, which opens through three French doors to a terrace and to the woods and fields beyond. Three of its four walls are made of field-stone, and its ceiling slopes upward to a window placed high in the wall above the main entrance. The dining room, shown on the lower left, features a bay of three triple-hung sash windows that come all the way down to the floor and are tall enough to walk out of when all the sashes are pushed up to the top. The photograph on the lower right shows the large indoor swimming pool, which is heated from solar collectors.

Kingsmill Housing

Like the house shown on the immediately preceding pages and Xanadune, shown on pages 84–87, this design for Kingsmill Housing, a new development near Williamsburg, Virginia, shows a tendency in Charles Moore's work during the 1970s to become more specific in its recollection of architectural shapes from the past. It is worth pointing out, though, and it is illustrated vividly in other projects from the same years, that this is only one of several tendencies, since Charles Moore's work has always been characterized by the variety of its surprises rather than by its single-mindedness.

It is also worth pointing out that though these designs are specific in their recalls, they are by no means verbatim. Has anyone ever seen before a dormer window like the one shown below and on the opposite page? Or corner pilasters on a Classic Revival house with trellises for their capitals? These are there to startle by their eccentricity, surely, but they are there also to please.

Kingsmill was designed in 1974 by Charles W. Moore Associates with Robert Harper, William Grover, and Glen Arbonies.

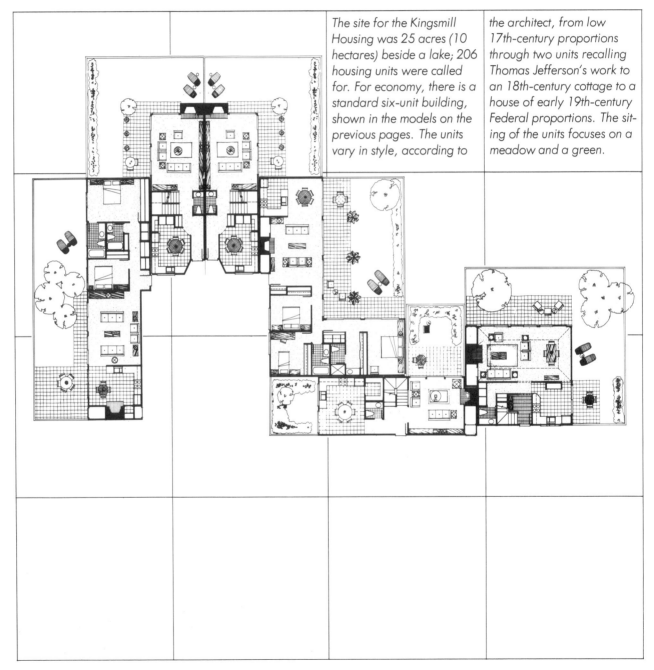

The site for the Kingsmill Housing was 25 acres (10 hectares) beside a lake; 206 housing units were called for. For economy, there is a standard six-unit building, shown in the models on the previous pages. The units vary in style, according to the architect, from low 17th-century proportions through two units recalling Thomas Jefferson's work to an 18th-century cottage to a house of early 19th-century Federal proportions. The siting of the units focuses on a meadow and a green.

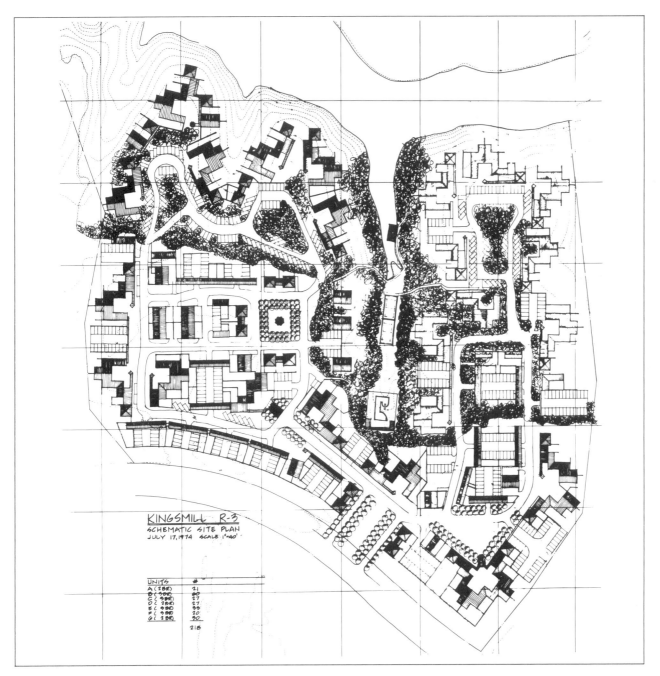

KINGSMILL R-3
SCHEMATIC SITE PLAN
JULY 17, 1974 SCALE 1"=40'

UNITS	#
A (2BR)	21
B (3BR)	80
C (3BR)	27
D (2BR)	27
E (4BR)	33
F (4BR)	20
G (2BR)	30
	218

Swan House

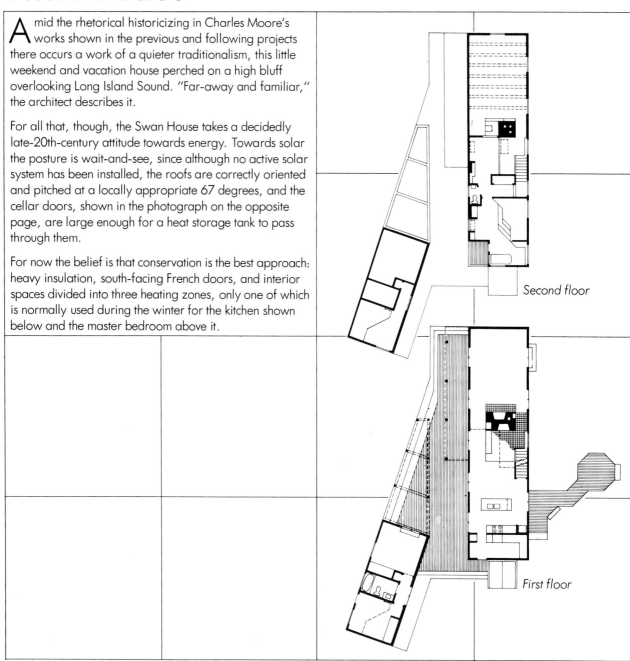

Amid the rhetorical historicizing in Charles Moore's works shown in the previous and following projects there occurs a work of a quieter traditionalism, this little weekend and vacation house perched on a high bluff overlooking Long Island Sound. "Far-away and familiar," the architect describes it.

For all that, though, the Swan House takes a decidedly late-20th-century attitude towards energy. Towards solar the posture is wait-and-see, since although no active solar system has been installed, the roofs are correctly oriented and pitched at a locally appropriate 67 degrees, and the cellar doors, shown in the photograph on the opposite page, are large enough for a heat storage tank to pass through them.

For now the belief is that conservation is the best approach: heavy insulation, south-facing French doors, and interior spaces divided into three heating zones, only one of which is normally used during the winter for the kitchen shown below and the master bedroom above it.

Second floor

First floor

The Swan House was designed by Moore Grover Harper with Mark Simon in 1975 and built in 1976. Beams from an old local barn were used throughout the house, as here in the living room where they become ties in the roof, stepping up and down with bands of African cloth stretched across them. The fireplace here as in the kitchen is air-circulating.

The living room is one heating zone, the kitchen and master bedroom above are a second, and the separate guest house is the third. In winter the living room is closed off from the rest of the house with 1-foot-thick (.3-meter) foam bats, which in summer become the furniture. The guest house is used infrequently during these months, and so the only spaces generally requiring heating are the kitchen and bedroom.

The bedroom of the Swan House features a bed on top of a platform reached by an elaborate set of stairs and an old-fashioned bathtub —a celebration, like the bath in Charles Moore's earlier house in Orinda, shown on pages 24—29, of the fact that bathing does not have to take place in a bathroom.

In summer the living spaces expand to the outdoors. The porch overhang, a trellis also made of old barn beams, and deciduous trees keep the house well shaded, while French doors provide cross ventilation.

Piazza d'Italia

The festive quality of Charles Moore's work is nowhere more evident than in the fountain he designed for the Piazza d'Italia. "Here," he says, "in a fountain built by New Orleans citizens of Italian descent, the contours form Italy. Sicily becomes a speaker's rostrum, and waters flow down the mirrored surfaces of the Arno, the Tiber, and the Po. The (Italian) classical orders of architecture appear, insofar as we could manage, in water, with volutes, acanthus leaves, flutes, and fillets, as well as egg-and-dart moldings all formed with jets. But the explicit references (if all this works) will only reinforce the excitement of the water, the marble, and the stainless steel, for the celebration is first of all one of the senses, and then for the mind and memory."[1]

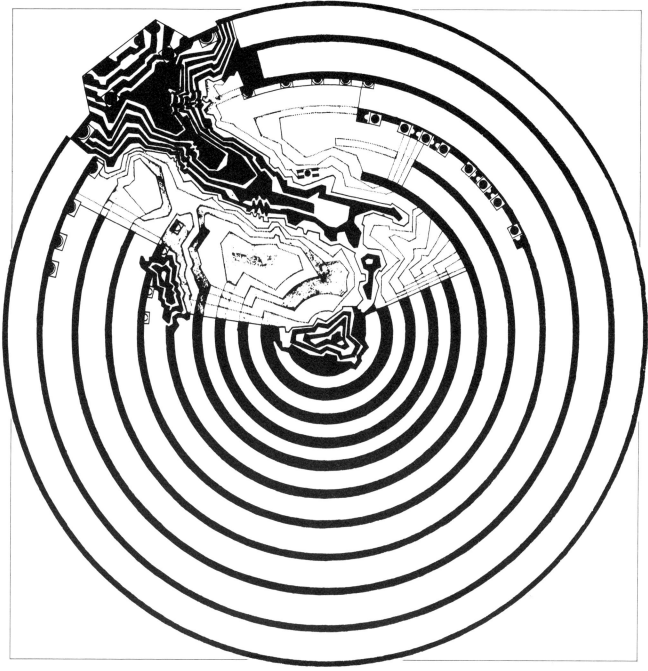

On St. Joseph's Day, March 19, altars in New Orleans are piled with food in honor of the patron saint, and the food is later distributed to the poor. The Piazza d'Italia fountain is designed as such an altar and also a place for general celebration, day and night, during the rest of the year.

The Piazza d'Italia fountain was designed in 1975 by Charles Moore and the Urban Innovations Group with Ron Filson, as well as with August Perez, Malcolm Heard, and Allen Eskew; Christine Beebe was the color consultant. The photograph on the left shows a part of the Piazza at night, and on the right is the entrance from the street.

Kuhio Shores Mauka

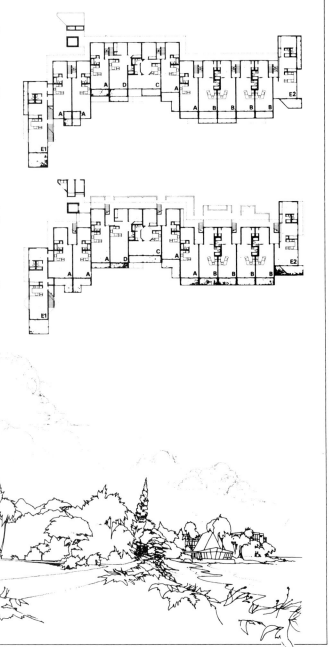

The program for this Hawaiian housing development called for 150 condominium apartments, mainly of one bedroom, all with an ocean view, and each with cross ventilation to catch the trade winds and make air conditioning unnecessary. Kuhio Shores Mauka consists of three identical buildings sited just behind a low shore road along the best surfing beach on the island of Kauai.

The buildings are four stories high, and for reasons of economy the lower one is of concrete block and the upper ones are wood frame. For all these practicalities, Kuhio Shores Mauka is remarkable—like Xanadune shown on pages 84—87, Kingsmill shown on pages 100—103, and, for that matter, like the Sea Ranch Condominium shown on pages 30—37—for the way a fairly standard late-20th-century housing program is cloaked in an image that is particular to a particular place. Charles Moore has said that a house should seem the center of the universe to its inhabitants. "Creating a center of the universe," he adds, "involves caring for what lies around, as well as in the minds of the future inhabitants."[1]

Kuhio Shores Mauka was designed in 1976 for a site on the island of Kauai in Hawaii by Charles Moore with MLTW/Turnbull Associates and the Urban Innovations Group. The photograph on the left shows the entrance side of one of the three identical buildings; the one below shows the side facing the ocean.

Best Products Showroom

Recently Best Products Company, the catalog-showroom merchandizer, commissioned six well-known American architects to design facades for their standard shopping-center buildings, and the results were shown early in 1980 with some fanfare at the Museum of Modern Art in New York. Most of the architects produced examples—rather predictable ones in many cases—of their current doctrinal persuasions. Charles Moore produced a facade of—what?—elephants carrying howdahs. There was, to be sure, a precedent if not an immediately evident reason. It was the Elephant Towers flanking the entrance to the 1939 Golden Gate International Exposition in San Francisco designed by the architectural firm Bakewell and Weihe and the sculptor Donald Macky.

Charles Moore's version copies the forms of the original surprisingly literally (they were fairly abstract to begin with) but renders them insubstantial by covering them with mirrors, so that they are only tantalizingly recognizable. Is it a joke, or is it a festive celebration like the Exposition was meant to be, or is it both?

The project was designed by Charles Moore and the Urban Innovations Group with Jim Winkler and Robert Flock.

Notes

Quotations from Charles Moore, when they have appeared in print, are cited in the notes below; otherwise they are from conversation and are quoted from memory.

ON THE ROAD TO THE PALACE OF WISDOM

1. Charles Moore and Gerald Allen, *Dimensions: space, shape & scale in architecture* (New York: Architectural Record Books, 1976), pp. 168–169.
2. Moore and Allen, *Dimensions*, p. 51.
3. *As You Like It*, II.i.15–17.
4. *A Midsummer Nights Dream*, IV.i.209–212.
5. *The Tempest*, IV.i.150.
6. Quoted by Charles Moore in "Personal Statement," *Architecture and Urbanism: The Work of Charles W. Moore 5* (May 1978), p. 11.
7. C.L. Barber, *Shakespeare's Festive Comedy: A Study of Dramatic Form and Its Relation to Social Custom* (Cleveland and New York: World Publishing Company, 1963).
8. Phillip Stubbes, *An Anatomie of Abuses . . . in Ailgna* (1583), ed. F.V. Furnival (London, 1877–1882), p. 149; quoted in Barber with modernized spelling, *Shakespeare's Festive Comedy*, p. 22.
9. William Empson, *Some Versions of Pastoral* (London: Chatto & Windus, 1950), pp. 27–86.
10. William Blake, "Proverbs of Hell," *The Marriage of Heaven and Hell*.

MOORE HOUSE, ORINDA

1. Charles Moore, Gerald Allen, Donlyn Lyndon, *The Place of Houses* (New York: Holt, Rinehart and Winston, 1974), p. 59.
2. Moore, Allen, Lyndon, *The Place of Houses*, pp. 51ff; also John Summerson, "Heavenly Mansions: An Interpretation of Gothic," *Heavenly Mansions* (New York: Norton, 1963), pp. 1–28.
3. Moore, Allen, Lyndon, *The Place of Houses*, p. 61.

SEA RANCH CONDOMINIUM

1. Quoted by Vincent Scully in "American Houses: Thomas Jefferson to Frank Lloyd Wright," *The Rise of an American Architecture*, ed. Edgar Kaufmann (New York, 1970), p. 184.
2. Charles Moore, Gerald Allen, Donlyn Lyndon, *The Place of Houses* (New York: Holt, Rinehart and Winston, 1974), p. 47.

SEA RANCH SWIM CLUB I

1. Edith Wharton and Ogden Codman, Jr., *The Decoration of Houses* (New York: W.W. Norton, 1978), p. 30.

MOORE HOUSE, NEW HAVEN

1. Charles Moore, Gerald Allen, Donlyn Lyndon, *The Place of Houses* (New York: Holt, Rinehart and Winston, 1974), p. 59.
2. C. Ray Smith, *Supermannerism: New Attitudes in Post-Modern Architecture* (New York, E.P. Dutton, 1977).
3. Charles Moore and Gerald Allen, *Dimensions: space, shape & scale in architecture* (New York: Architectural Record Books, 1976), p. 10.

CHURCH STREET SOUTH

1. Charles Moore, "Housing," *Architecture and Urbanism: The Work of Charles W. Moore 5* (May 1978), p. 181.

SANTA BARBARA FACULTY CLUB

1. Charles Moore, "Celebrations," *Architecture and Urbanism: The Work of Charles W. Moore 5* (May 1978), p. 251.

Credits

MOORE HOUSE, CENTERBROOK

1. Charles Moore, Gerald Allen, Donlyn Lyndon, *The Place of Houses* (New York: Holt, Rinehart and Winston, 1974), pp. 226, 229.
2. Moore, Allen, Lyndon, *The Place of Houses*, p. 225.

PIAZZA D'ITALIA

1. Charles Moore, "Celebrations," *Architecture and Urbanism: The Work of Charles W. Moore* 5 (May 1978), p. 252.

KUHIO SHORES MAUKA

1. Charles Moore, "Housing," *Architecture and Urbanism: The Work of Charles W. Moore* 5 (May 1978), p. 184.

Chronology

1925
Born in Benton Harbor,
Michigan

1942
Graduated from Lakeview High
School, Battle Creek, Michigan

1946
Jones Cottage (built in 1947)
Torch Lake, Michigan

1947
Bachelor of Architecture,
University of Michigan

1947–1949
Worked in offices of Mario
Corbett, Joseph Allen Stein,
and Clark and Beuttler,
San Francisco

1949
Jones House (project)
Eugene, Oregon

1949–1950
George Booth Travelling
Fellowship in Europe and the
Near East

1950–1952
Assistant Professor of
Architecture,
University of Utah,
Salt Lake City

1952–1954
Lieutenant, U.S. Army Corps of
Engineers in the United
States, Japan, and Korea

1953
Weingarten House
(constructed in 1953)
Pebble Beach, California

1954
Kahn House (project)
Carmel Highlands, California

Arnold House (project)
Carmel, California

Farr Professional Building
(project)
Seaside, California

Moore House (project)
Pebble Beach, California

1956
Master of Fine Arts,
Princeton University

Seaside Professional
Building I (built in 1956)
Seaside, California

Stores and Offices (project)
Seaside, California

Twohig House (built in 1956)
Monterey, California

Weingarten House Addition
and Alteration (built in 1956)
Pebble Beach, California

1957
Doctor of Philosophy,
Princeton University

Seaside Jewish Community
Center (project)
Seaside, California

Hubbard House I
(built in 1957)
Monterey, California

1958
Council of the Humanities
Post-Doctoral Fellowship,
Princeton University

Matterson House
(built in 1959)
Monterey, California
With William Turnbull

Seaside Professional
Building II (built in 1959)
Seaside, California

1958–1959
Assistant Professor,
Princeton University

1959
Hubbard House II
(built in 1960)
Corral de Tierra, California
With Richard C. Peters

1959–1962
Associate Professor,
University of California
at Berkeley

Worked individually and in
offices of Clark and Beuttler,
San Francisco

1961
Paston Porte Cochère
(built in 1961)
Los Angeles, California

Bonham House (built in 1962)
Boulder Creek, California
With Warren Fuller

Jenkins House I (project)
St. Helena, California

Jobson House (built in 1961)
Palo Colorado Canyon,
California

1962
Moore House (built in 1962)
Orinda, California

Otus Houses I, II, and III
(III built in 1962)
Berkeley, California
With Warren Fuller

West Plaza Condominium
(project)
Coronado, California
With Donlyn Lyndon
and William Turnbull

Citizens Federal Savings and
Loan Building (built in 1963)
San Francisco, California
For Clark Beuttler Architects

Cortese House (project)
Orinda, California

1962–1965
Chairman,
Department of Architecture,
University of California
at Berkeley

Worked with MLTW (Moore
Lyndon Turnbull Whitaker),
Berkeley, California

1963
Fremont Professional Center

(built in 1963)
Fremont, California
With MLTW

Jewell House (built in 1963)
Orinda, California
With MLTW

Monte Vista Apartments
(built in 1963)
Monterey, California
With MLTW

Turner-Hall House (project)
Pebble Beach, California
With MLTW

Jenkins House II
(built in 1963)
St. Helena, California
With MLTW

1964

Cudaback House Remodeling
(project)
Oakland, California
With MLTW

Sea Ranch Condominium I
(built in 1965)
Sea Ranch, California
With MLTW

Slater House (built in 1964)
Stinson Beach, California
With MLTW

Talbert House (built in 1964)
Oakland, California
With MLTW

Seaside Professional
Building II (built in 1964)
Seaside, California
With MLTW

1965

Alcoa Pre-Fab Housing
(project)
With MLTW/Moore-Turnbull

Carmel Knolls Housing
(project)
Carmel, California
With MLTW/Moore-Turnbull

Johnson House (built in 1966)
Sea Ranch, California
With MLTW/Moore-Turnbull

Karas House (built in 1966)
Monterey, California
With MLTW/Moore-Turnbull

Lawrence House (built in 1966)
Sea Ranch, California
With MLTW/Moore-Turnbull

Portland South Park Lovejoy
Fountain (built in 1966)
Portland, Oregon
With MLTW/Moore-Turnbull
as consultants to Lawrence
Halprin & Associates

1965–1969

Chairman,
Department of Architecture,
Yale University

Worked with MLTW/Moore-
Turnbull,
New Haven, Connecticut,
and San Francisco,
California

1965–1972

Kresge College, University of
California at Santa Cruz
(built in 1974)
Santa Cruz, California

With MLTW/Moore-Turnbull
and Marvin Buchanan, Robert
Calderwood, Robert Simpson,
and Richard C. Peters
(lighting consultant)

1966

Sea Ranch Athletic Club I
(built in 1966)
Sea Ranch, California
With MLTW/Moore-Turnbull;
pool and tennis court by
Lawrence Halprin & Associates;
graphics by Barbara
Stauffacher

Thomasian House
(built in 1966)
Orinda, California
With MLTW/Moore-Turnbull

Sea Ranch Corporation Yard
(built in 1966)
Sea Ranch, California
With MLTW/Moore-Turnbull

Harrison House (project)
Santa Barbara, California
With MLTW/Moore-Turnbull

Moore House Renovation
(built in 1966)
New Haven, Connecticut
With MLTW/Moore-Turnbull

Savin Rock Urban Renewal
Project No. 2 (project)
New Haven, Connecticut
With MLTW/Moore-Turnbull

Faculty Club, University of
California at Santa Barbara
(built in 1968)
Santa Barbara, California
With MLTW/Moore-Turnbull
and Donlyn Lyndon, Marvin

Buchanan, and Bruce Beebe

Boas House (built in 1967)
Stinson Beach, California
With MLTW/Moore-Turnbull

Bransten House Remodeling
(project)
San Francisco, California
With MLTW/Moore-Turnbull

Budge House (built in 1967)
Healdsburg, California
With MLTW/Moore-Turnbull

Halprin House (built in 1966)
Sea Ranch, California
With MLTW/Moore Turnbull

Knutsen House (built in 1966)
Sonoma, California
With MLTW/Moore-Turnbull

Saltzman House (built in 1966)
Carmel, California
With MLTW/Moore-Turnbull

Sea Ranch Condominium,
Hillside Unit (project)
Sea Ranch, California
With MLTW/Moore-Turnbull

Akron Cascade Urban Renewal
(project)
Akron, Ohio
With MLTW/Moore-Turnbull in
joint venture with Lawrence
Halprin & Associates

1966–1968

Church Street South Moderate
Income Housing (built in 1969)
New Haven, Connecticut
With MLTW/Moore-Turnbull
and Marvin Buchanan and
Donald Whitaker

1967

Bankes House (project)
Brewster, New York
With MLTW/Moore-Turnbull

Seaside Elderly Housing
(built in 1967)
Seaside, California
With MLTW/Moore-Turnbull
and Sabastian Bordonaro
Associates

Pirofski House (project)
Palo Alto, California
With MLTW/Moore-Turnbull

Sea Ranch Barn Houses
(built in 1967–1969)
Sea Ranch, California
With MLTW/Moore-Turnbull

1967–1968

Tower One, Jewish Community
Council Housing
(built in 1970)
New Haven, Connecticut
With MLTW/Moore-Turnbull
and Marvin Buchanan, Edward
Johnson, and Mary Ann
Rumney

Klotz House (built in 1970)
Westerly, Rhode Island
With MLTW/Moore-Turnbull
and William Grover and
Marvin Buchanan

1968

Shinefield House
(built in 1968–1976)
San Francisco, California
With Dmitri Vedensky

Shinefield House
(built in 1970–1977)

Sea Ranch, California
With Dmitri Vedensky

Tri-Pac Housing (project)
Vernon, Connecticut
With MLTW/Moore-Turnbull

Navy Lodge Officers Housing
(project)
New London, Connecticut, and
Newport, Rhode Island
With MLTW/Moore-Turnbull
and Larry Linder

New Haven College Student
Housing (project)
New Haven, Connecticut
With MLTW/Moore-Turnbull

Pearson House Addition
(built in 1969)
Branford, Connecticut
With MLTW/Moore-Turnbull
and Steven Izenour

Tempchin House (built in 1969)
Bethesda, Maryland
With MLTW/Moore-Turnbull
and Rik Ekstrom

University of Connecticut
Staff Housing (project)
Storrs, Connecticut
With MLTW/Moore-Turnbull

Robert T. Wolfe Elderly
Housing (built in 1970)
New Haven, Connecticut
With MLTW/Moore-Turnbull
and Robert Harper and
Marvin Buchanan

Wooster Street Housing
and Commercial (project)
New Haven, Connecticut
With MLTW/Moore-Turnbull

Psychoanalytic Associates
Office Building

(built in 1971)
Los Angeles, California
With MLTW/Moore-Turnbull
and Arthur Ballman and
Richard Chylinski

Sea Ranch Spec House (project)
Sea Ranch, California
With MLTW/Moore-Turnbull

Weyerhauser Demonstration
House (built in 1969)
Kansas City, Missouri
With MLTW/Moore-Turnbull

1969

American Shakespeare Theatre
(project)
Stratford, Connecticut
With MLTW/Moore-Turnbull

Cornuelle House (project)
New Hampshire
With MLTW/Moore-Turnbull

Eastern Kentucky Housing
Development Corporation
(project)
Whitesburg, Kentucky
With MLTW/Moore-Turnbull
and Ron Filson and
Thomas Rapp

Essex Point Housing I
(project)
Deep River, Connecticut
With MLTW/Moore-Turnbull

Gagarin House
(built in 1971–1972)
Peru, Vermont
With MLTW/Moore-Turnbull
and Arthur Ballman

Koizim House (built in 1971)
Westport, Connecticut
With MLTW/Moore-Turnbull

and Arthur Ballman

Murray House Renovation
(built in 1970–1975)
Cambridge, Massachusetts
With Charles W. Moore
Associates

Orono Housing (built in 1971)
Orono, Maine
With Charles W. Moore
Associates and Marvin
Buchanan and Robert Harper

Saz House (built in 1971)
Woods Hole, Massachusetts
With Charles W. Moore
Associates

Schub House (project)
Sag Harbor, New York
With MLTW/Moore-Turnbull

Stern House (built in 1970)
Woodbridge, Connecticut
With Charles W. Moore
Associates

Sea Ranch Athletic Club II
(built in 1971)
Sea Ranch, California
With MLTW/Turnbull
Associates and Donlyn Lyndon;
graphics by Martha and
Jerry Wagner

1969–1970

Dean, School of Architecture
and Planning, Yale University

1970

Essex Point, Scheme II
(project)
Deep River, Connecticut
With Charles W. Moore
Associates and Larry Linder

and Marvin Buchanan

Goodman House, Schemes I—V (project)
Montauk, New York
With Charles W. Moore Associates

Main Street Partnership, stores and offices (partially built in 1971)
Essex, Connecticut
With Charles W. Moore Associates

Maplewood Terrace Low-Income Housing (built in 1971)
Middletown, Connecticut
With Charles W. Moore Associates and Frank Gravino

Middletown Inn and Renewal (project)
Middletown, Connecticut
With Charles W. Moore Associates and Robert Benfro

Middletown Low-Rent Elderly Housing (project)
Middletown, Connecticut
With Charles W. Moore Associates

Moore House (project)
Essex, Connecticut
With Charles W. Moore Associates and Marvin Buchanan

Moore House Renovation (built in 1971—1975)
Essex, Connecticut
With Charles W. Moore Associates and Mary Ann Rumney and Thomas Dryer

Rudolph House (built in 1971)

Captiva Island, Florida
With Charles W. Moore Associates and James V. Righter
Southern Illinois University (project)
Carbondale, Illinois
With Charles W. Moore Associates

Station Plaza (project)
Huntington, New York
With Charles W. Moore Associates and Gilbert Hoffman

Worcester Polytechnic Institute (project)
Worcester, Massachusetts
With Charles W. Moore Associates and Don Whitaker

1970—1975

Professor, School of Architecture, Yale University

1971

Clarke House (built in 1971)
Old Lyme, Connecticut
With Charles W. Moore Associates and William Grover

Heritage Harbour (project)
Annapolis, Maryland
With Charles W. Moore Associates

Klotz Development (project)
Westhampton Beach, New York
With Charles W. Moore Associates

Margra's Drive-In (built in 1973)
New London, Connecticut
With Charles W. Moore

Associates and Robert Harper

McCall's House (built in 1972)
Ocala, Florida
With Charles W. Moore Associates

Orlando Housing (project)
Orlando, Florida
With Charles W. Moore Associates

RAVAL Planning Study
Huntington, New York
With Charles W. Moore Associates

Whitman Village Housing (built in 1975)
Huntington, New York
With Charles W. Moore Associates and Robert Harper

Taylor Townhouses (built in 1972)
Norwalk, Connecticut
With Charles W. Moore Associates and William Grover, Robert Harper, and Mary Ann Rumney

1972

Ambro House, Schemes I—II (built in 1973)
East Hampton, New York
With Charles W. Moore Associates and Robert Harper

Antioch College, South Hall (project)
Yellow Springs, Ohio
With Charles W. Moore Associates

Burns House (built in 1974)
Santa Monica, California
With Richard Chylinski; colors

by Christine Beebe; lighting by Richard C. Peters

Chester Diversified Properties (project)
Chester, Connecticut
With Charles W. Moore Associates

Dauntless Yacht Club (project)
Essex, Connecticut
With Charles W. Moore Associates and Carl Wies

E.M.I. Reception Center (project)
St. Simons Island, Georgia
With Charles W. Moore Associates

Essex Point, Scheme III (project)
Deep River, Connecticut
With Charles W. Moore Associates and Carl Wies, Robert Harper, and Robert Yudell

Hindman Pool (project)
New Zion, Kentucky
With Charles W. Moore Associates and Thomas Dryer

Indian Springs Ranch (project)
Salinas, California
With Charles W. Moore Associates and Thomas Dryer

Malibu Apartments (project)
Malibu, California
With Charles W. Moore Associates and Richard Chylinski

Xanadune (project)
St. Simons Island, Georgia
With Charles W. Moore Associates and Richard Oliver,

Mary Ann Rumney, and
Robert Yudell

1972–1973

Kansas City Graphics
(partially built in 1973)
Kansas City, Kansas
With Charles W. Moore
Associates and Mary Ann
Rumney and Thomas Dryer

1973

Anderson Housing
Development (project)
Springfield, Massachusetts
With Charles W. Moore
Associates and Thomas Dryer

County Federal Savings Bank
(built in 1973)
Greens Farms, Connecticut
With Charles W. Moore
Associates and William
Grover, Mary Ann Rumney,
and Richard Oliver

House near New York
(built in 1976)
With Richard Oliver

Levin House (built in 1974)
Little Falls, New York
With Charles W. Moore
Associates and Marvin
Buchanan and Jefferson Riley

Old Farm (project)
Mt. Holly, New Jersey
With Charles W. Moore
Associates and Richard Oliver
and Wing Hung Wong

1974

Barber House (built in 1976)

Guilford, Connecticut
With Charles W. Moore
Associates and Richard Oliver;
colors by Christine Beebe

Doll House, Tuscan
With Charles W. Moore
Associates and Robert Harper

Doll House, Castle
With Robert Yudell and
Christine Beebe

Kingsmill Housing (project)
Williamsburg, Virginia
With Charles W. Moore
Associates and Robert Harper,
William Grover, and Glen
Arbonies

Madras Consulate-General's
Residence Renovation
(built in 1975)
Madras, India
With Charles W. Moore
Associates and Jefferson Riley

Owen Brown Village (project)
Columbia, Maryland
With MLTW/Turnbull
Associates and Charles W.
Moore Associates

Stonington Development
(project)
Stonington, Connecticut
With Charles W. Moore
Associates

Taft-Adams Renovation
(project)
New Haven, Connecticut
With Charles W. Moore
Associates and Edward
Johnson and J.P.C. Floyd

Temple of Understanding

(project)
St. Mary's County, Maryland
With Charles W. Moore
Associates

Paumanack Manor Elderly
Housing (project)
Huntington, New York
With Charles W. Moore
Associates

1975

Cold Springs Harbor
Laboratories, Waste Treatment
Building,
Airslie House, Jones
Laboratory, and Cancer
Laboratories
(built in 1976–1977)
Cold Springs Harbor,
New York
With Moore Grover Harper

Cranbury Road Housing
(project)
Hightstown, New Jersey
With Moore Grover Harper

Piazza d'Italia Fountain
(built in 1977–1978)
New Orleans, Louisiana
With Urban
Innovations Group and Ron
Filson, August Perez, Malcolm
Heard, and Allen Eskew; colors
by Christine Beebe

Swan House (built in 1976)
Southhold, New York
Moore Grover Harper
and Mark Simon

Moore Rogger Hofflander
Condominium (built in 1978)
Los Angeles, California
With Richard Chylinski

Heady House, addition for
former Moore House (project)
Orinda, California
With Urban Innovations Group
and Ron Filson and John Ruble

Riverdesign Dayton (project)
Dayton, Ohio
With Moore Grover Harper,
Lorenz and Williams, and
J.P.C. Floyd

Norwich Armed Forces Reserve
Center (built in 1978)
Norwich, Connecticut
With Moore Grover Harper
and Arthur D. Little

Abel House (built in 1978)
Los Angeles, California
With Urban Innovations Group
and Ron Fink and Robert Yudell

Kuhio Shores Mauka (project)
Kauai, Hawaii
With MLTW/Turnbull
Associates
and Urban Innovations Group

Rodes House (built in 1979)
Los Angeles, California
With Robert Yudell

Isham House (built in 1977)
Sagaponak, New York
With Moore Grover Harper
and Mark Simon

Rubenstein House
(built in 1977)
Trappe, Maryland
With Moore Grover Harper
and Mark Simon; landscape by
Lester Collins

1975 to present

Professor, University of

California at Los Angeles, and
Visiting Professor, School of
Architecture, Yale University

1977

Licht House (built in 1978)
Mill Valley, California
With Urban Innovations Group
and Nicholas Pyle

Minnesota II State Capitol
Competition (project)
St. Paul, Minnesota
With William Turnbull, Ron
Filson, Barton Phelps, and
Nicholas Pyle

Wilheim House (project)
Woodland Hills, California
With Urban Innovations Group
and Elias Torres and
John Ruble

Larson House (project)
Angwin, California
With Robert Yudell

Meyer Duplexes (project)
Redondo Beach, California

1978

RPI Fountain (project)
Troy, New York
With Moore Grover Harper
and William Grover and
Jefferson Riley

Stanwood House (built in 1979)
Bloomfield, Connecticut
With Moore Grover Harper
and Mark Simon

1979

Roanoke Design 79 (project)

Roanoke, Virginia
With Moore Grover Harper
and J.P.C. Floyd

Gundwin Offices (built in 1980)
Princeton, New Jersey
With Moore Grover Harper
and Mark Simon